Thanks to Christien Vandeputte.

Copyright © 2021 Clavis Publishing Inc., New York

Originally published as *De verpleegkundige* in Belgium and the Netherlands by Clavis Uitgeverij, 2011
English translation from the Dutch by Clavis Publishing Inc., New York

Visit us on the Web at www.clavis-publishing.com.

Nurses and What They Do written and illustrated by Liesbet Slegers

ISBN 978-1-60537-713-1

This book was printed in June 2022 at Nikara, M. R. Štefánika 858/25, 963 01 Krupina, Slovakia.

First Edition
10 9 8 7 6 5 4 3 2

Clavis Publishing supports the First Amendment and celebrates the right to read.

Nurses
and What They Do

Liesbet Slegers

Clavis

NEW YORK

When you are sick or hurting, you sometimes have to go to the hospital. There, someone takes care of you. That's the job of a nurse. Nurses help people bathe, they give medicine, and they help with surgery. Some nurses also help people at home. Some of their patients include older people who can't take care of themselves anymore.

watch

Many nurses wear scrubs, loose fitting clothing worn by hospital staff. Sometimes they wear medical gloves when they have to treat patients. Nurses use their watch to measure how fast a patient's heart is beating and to see when they need to give someone a pill or an injection. On their feet, they wear comfortable shoes because nurses walk all over hospitals and doctors' offices all day long.

washing basin

Nurses need many things. On their cart, they put the medicine they bring to each patient. A patient is someone who is in the hospital or at the doctor's office because they're sick. On the cart are syringes, disinfectant, and many other things. They also use a thermometer and a sphygmomanometer to see if patients have a fever or monitor their blood pressure. In the morning, patients need to be bathed. Some can do it themselves, and sometimes sick people need help getting out of bed. So, a nurse will help them.

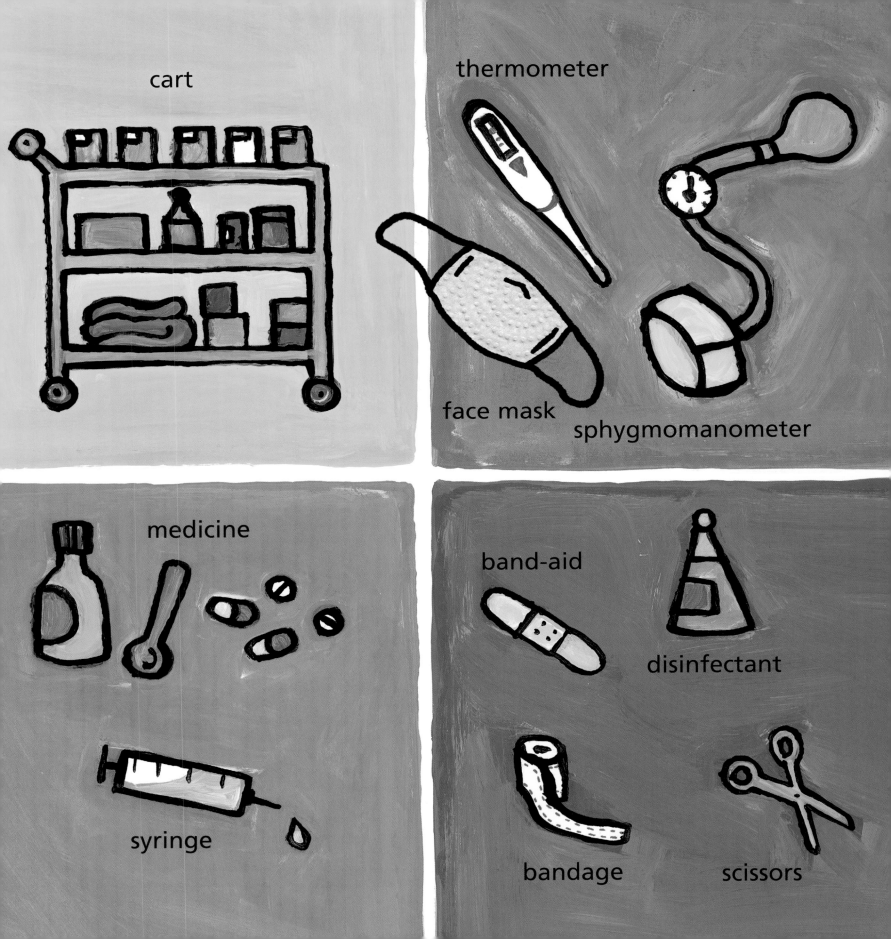

When you walk through the hospital doors, you see many rooms. In those rooms are the sick patients. They need care from the nurses all day. Nurses work early in the morning, or late in the evening. They even work at night.

Look, the nurse who has been working all night long can go home now. He has worked hard and deserves to get some rest. Before he leaves, he tells the other nurse what has happened that night: the doctor has brought in a boy with a high fever. He's in room 321. When the new nurse knows all this, she can take care of the boy too.

First, the nurse washes her hands very carefully. They must be clean before she goes to help someone. Then she prepares the cart by putting medicine for the patients on it. All the patients have their own box of medicine with their room number and name on it.
The doctor has told the nurse who needs medicine. On her computer, she can check to make sure the patients get the right medicine.
At the bottom of the cart are other things she needs to take care of the patients. Now she can start her shift.

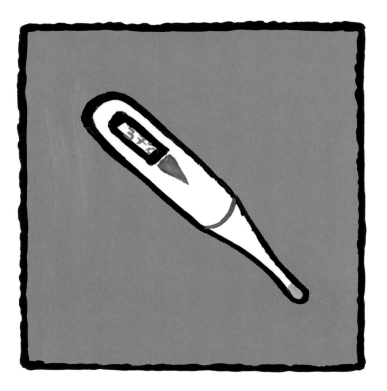

Soon she arrives at the room of the boy who has been
brought in overnight.

"Good morning, I'm your nurse. How are you doing?" she asks kindly.

"I already feel a bit better," the boy says, "I hope I can go home soon."

"When the doctor comes, he'll tell you when you can go,"
the nurse answers.

The nurse takes the boy's temperature. Then she puts the inflatable
cuff around his upper arm and presses a button. The cuff is tight now.
When the machine is finished, the cuff is loose again.

"Your blood pressure is fine, and your fever is almost gone!"

In the meantime, another patient has pressed the alarm button.
This button hangs close to the bed, and sick people can always reach it.
When someone needs something, and the nurse isn't around,
the patient can push it to call one. As fast as she can, the nurse
goes to the room.

The nurse enters the room.

"Good morning, can I help you?" she asks kindly.

"My leg is hurting so much," the girl says.

"Maybe it'll be better if I help you sit up in bed and put another pillow underneath your leg," the nurse suggests. "I'll ask the doctor if I can give you something to help with the pain."

The nurse and the doctor discuss how the patients are doing.
Does anyone feel bad? Or better? Does anyone need
medicine to help with the pain? The nurse informs the doctor.
When they talk about the girl in pain, the doctor knows exactly
which medicine she should take to feel better.

An old lady needs an injection.

She has to get it every day at eleven o' clock.

"I see you have received a gift!" the nurse says.

"These are chocolates. My daughter bought them for me.

Sweet, isn't it?"

The nurse gives the lady an injection. It's done in no time.

She sees the lady is already feeling better than she was yesterday.

The doctor has decided the boy who had a fever can go home.
The boy has a surprise for the nurse: he gives her a lovely postcard.
"Thank you for taking such good care of me," he says. "You always
knew what I needed. Can I become a nurse when I'm older?"
"Of course!" the nurse laughs. She gives him a letter with instructions
for the medicine he must take at home. She says goodbye and goes
to the next patient.

Nurses can work in a hospital, but they can also do other work.

They help the elderly who can't take care of themselves anymore and live in a **nursing home**. Nurses not only take care of them by giving them medicine, but they also talk to the older people.

During **surgery**, a doctor can use some helping hands. Nurses may assist the doctor or arrange the tools the doctor will use for surgery.

Sometimes **babies** are so sick they have to go to the hospital for a while. Nurses not only give them medicine, but they also wash and feed them. Look, this baby is already feeling a lot better.

When someone doesn't have to stay in a hospital but still needs to be taken care of, nurses may visit them **at home**. That way, the patient can get better. We appreciate our nurses!